BTAC
BSTO
1

Y629.2222 E57 1970   (3)
Engel, L.K.
  132 of the most unusual cars that ever ran at Indianapolis

TULSA CITY-COUNTY LIBRARY SYSTEM
Tulsa, Oklahoma

Any resident of Tulsa County may borrow books.

A fine must be paid for each book kept overtime (Sundays and holidays included).

Books may be returned to any library agency in Tulsa County.

132
OF THE MOST
UNUSUAL CARS
THAT EVER RAN
AT INDIANAPOLIS

132
OF THE MOST UNUSUAL CARS THAT EVER RAN AT INDIANAPOLIS

Produced by Lyle Kenyon Engel
and the Editors of Auto Racing magazine

ARCO PUBLISHING COMPANY, INC.
New York

Photography
George Engel
Indianapolis Motor Speedway
Bud Jones

Editorial Staff
Ross R. Olney
George Engel
Marla Ray

An index of cars and drivers appears on page 157.

Published by ARCO PUBLISHING COMPANY, INC.
219 Park Avenue South, New York, N.Y. 10003
Copyright © Lyle Kenyon Engel, 1970
All Rights Reserved
Library of Congress Catalog Number 72-103077
ISBN 0-668-02194-2
Printed in the United States of America
Typography by Elroy

Introduction

This collection of material on the most innovative cars to appear at Indianapolis is long overdue. It should be of interest not only to racing people but to all students of our country's automotive history.

For me, the unusual cars at Indy have always been the important cars. And logically enough, they have seldom been the winning cars. Brand-new ideas require much time for testing, but innovation—the act of striking into new frontiers—has always been the real name of the game in automobile racing, which to me is a logical and necessary extension of the profession of engineering.

No indeed, the "far-out cars" of Indianapolis have almost never appeared in Victory Lane—at least not until the ideas contained in their design had ceased to be really new. The names of those cars and their designers are seldom hailed at the victory banquets and are mentioned all too seldom in the literature of racing, which naturally enough is pretty well confined to the accomplishments of winners.

But the innovators in automobile racing have made their contributions, sometimes quietly and almost without notice, and sometimes (as in my case) with a good deal of sound and fury. The list is long and some of them contained in this book may surprise you. Others, such as the pioneering front-drive cars, the great diesel engine adventure, those wonderful ear-splitting Novis, first roadster designs, my own ill-fated Turbocars, are all a great and well-known part of the Indianapolis story.

I am proud indeed to have more than one of my own cars included in this group of truly unusual racing machinery. Although we at STP Corporation were able to win the 1969 race with Mario Andretti in a car of conservative and normal design, I still look forward to the day when we can bring a car to victory in the "500" that properly belongs on the list of truly innovative vehicles. That is our next goal, and today I feel more confident than ever of its achievement.

Anthony (Andy) Granatelli
Director, STP Racing Team

The Indianapolis "500"

Indianapolis, Indiana, exists pretty much out of the mind of man for 11 months each year. Rarely does anything of major significance occur there and carry to the outside world. The city is a typical Midwestern community, concerned with itself and its own problems, and unconcerned about what the outside world thinks unless these thoughts relate to Indianapolis. It sails along like a huge ocean liner on the calm sea of Indiana's lush, flat farmlands.

But then, once each year, the ocean liner is plunged into a great hurricane. Everything that happens in Indianapolis is of concern to the outside world, particularly the sports world. If a drop of rain falls, it is of significance. The temperature of the day, for almost an entire month, is important. As the month of May progresses, more and more people arrive at the Indianapolis airport, and by train to the downtown station, and by car and truck and bus. Major newswires are set up, and the Indianapolis newspapers, who normally wouldn't ship beyond the suburbs except for mailings to Indianapolis-bred servicemen overseas, expand their circulation-by-mail to the entire world.

For, during the month of May, and particularly on Memorial Day, people are interested in what is happening in Indianapolis.

Why? Because on Memorial Day, after a full month of preparation, at a track northwest of downtown Indianapolis, a motor race unlike any other in the world is held. It is a race of world champions, the best in the business, a race of the very finest cars in the world, a race for the largest single purse in all of sports, a race that can make a man wealthy beyond his wildest dreams, a race of great pomp and circumstance and tradition, a race which draws the greatest mass of spectators in all of sports, a race which must be seen to be believed.

Not many realize it any more with the dominance of Detroit, but Indianapolis was once the center of the automotive world. In this city were built many new cars, and many accessory companies did business in Indianapolis. So it was natural that a great test track should be built. The first man to have the idea was Carl Fisher who, in 1908, was a partner with Jim Allison in the Prest-O-Lite Company, a manufacturer of carbide lamps for automobiles. Fisher and Allison arranged the group which originally financed the purchase of land and construction of facilities, work which got underway in 1909.

A rectangular shape had been selected for the track, and construction materials of crushed stone and asphalt. The track was to be two and one half miles in length, with four turns each a quarter of a mile long. These turns would be joined by two long straightaways of five-eighths of a mile and by two shorter ones of one eighth of a mile. The track was completed in time for a series of auto races on August 19, 1909.

But the track broke up badly during the afternoon, causing the deaths of one driver, two riding mechanics and two spectators. The management realized that the entire track needed a better surface, and so bricks, the best known surface of the day, were chosen. Sixty-three hard days later the entire track had been bricked.

Exhibition races were held on December 17 and 18, 1909, and on May 27, 1910, the latter a series of events from five to 200 miles. Sixty thousand spectators filled the stands for the May 27 races. Further programs were held on July 4th and Labor Day weekends.

Then the management of the successful new Indianapolis Motor Speedway made a major decision. Henceforth the track would be used only once each year for a racing event, with the rest of the year devoted to testing of cars and automotive accessories. The decision has held to this day. Memorial Day was chosen as the day for the yearly event, which was to be a 500-mile race. The first would be held in 1911 for the then-unheard of purse of $25,000.

The first 500-mile race was an unqualified success from the standpoint of fans and management and drivers, and the tradition began. They didn't qualify for that first race . . . not as we know qualification, at any rate. They filled starting positions in the order their entries came in, with only one provision. Each car had to be able to run a quarter of a mile at better than 75 miles per hour. Piston displacement was limited to a huge 500 cubic inches. Forty cars thundered away in smoke and sound in that first race, and the winner was Ray Harroun in a Marmon Wasp. His winning speed was 74.59 miles per hour.

Yes, Harroun rode alone (the others carried riding mechanics) and yes, he had fashioned a glass prism on a metal framework over his cockpit so that he could see to the rear. Yes, this was the first use of the rear view mirror, now found on all passenger cars.

Far more important, this was only one of many automotive innovations first tested and proved at the Indianapolis Motor Speedway and ultimately used on passenger cars.

This is not to say that the primary purpose of the great Indianapolis Speedway Race is automotive development. It is not. The race is a fantastically exciting sporting event which draws nearly 300,000 fans to the track and millions more around the world on closed-circuit television. They come, and they watch, to see a great competitive event. But a natural result of mechanics' attempts to prepare a car perfectly for a killing 500-mile grind at top speeds is development of newer and better-performing automotive parts. It can't help but be.

Consider tires, for example. What better testing ground than this torturous race? And the results? Over the years tires have been improved from the point where they were the major cause of pit stops and accidents to the point where they are now almost ignored. The entire race is easily run on one set of tires, and negligible wear shows at the end. These fine developments have been passed on to the same manufacturer's passenger car tires . . . even to the point of naming them with such names as "The 500" and the like.

The great Wilbur Shaw, three-time winner of the "500" and finally President of the Speedway, said in 1949, "Greater safety, comfort, economy and dependability will be new features on future passenger cars as the result of the annual 500-mile automobile race at the Indianapolis Motor Speedway this year."

Then Shaw went on to point out improved carburetors and fuel injectors, new suspension systems, superchargers and other experiments on racers which, true to his prediction, have since appeared on passenger cars in modified forms. Engineers have always turned to Indy for testing, for they have become convinced that the 500 miles an Indianapolis racer runs (if it runs that far, that is) is equal to 50,000 miles on an American highway. And, true to Fisher's original idea, the track is used year around by automotive engineers for testing new devices and ideas. Only that period when snow covers the Midwest each year is the track closed, and engineers are eagerly waiting in line each year for the thaw to begin.

Spark plugs are another device constantly being tested under racing conditions. Fuels are still another, since the first use of ethyl gasoline at Indy by Tommy Milton in 1923 . . . when he raised the track record by more than seven miles per hour using "high test" gasoline. More currently, twin overhead cam engines have been tested and proven at the "500," unique four-wheel independent suspensions, four-wheel drives, disc brakes and better instrumentation are race tested and proven. Stock block engines are now being used in racing cars, and the resulting improvements are passed directly back to passenger cars.

In fact, with the current involvement of engineers directly from the companies in the passenger car manufacturing business, and their work in the pits at Indy, and considering that many racers are now using engines from "standard" passenger car builders (albeit special racing models), the very thoughts of manufacturers are tuned to racing. In the past several years such companies as Buick, Chevrolet, Studebaker, Plymouth, Dodge, turbine manufacturers and others and certainly the Ford Motor Company, have directly participated not only at Indy on race day and throughout the year, but in other forms of racing as well.

Goodyear, Firestone and several other tire companies, even the venerable Sears Roebuck and Co., have participated in elaborate testing programs at the track and in the 500-mile race. Many major accessory companies are in evidence throughout the year, and on race day, testing their products on racing cars. The cars have become billboards of advertising with the insistence of proud manufacturers to have their names boldly shown on the cars for all to see . . . and heavy accessory prize money is awarded to drivers using these products in the race.

There is no longer any reticence on the part of most automotive manufacturers to have their names connected to auto racing. With the continually growing popularity of auto racing, which has become the second largest spectator sport in the country, there is a fond desire on the part of auto parts manufacturers to become associated with the sport. But this forces them to improve their parts to the point where they will last throughout the long grind, for any part that fails is just as highly publicized as those parts which do not fail. The pressure, then, is on the manufacturer. He wants to play the game, so he is forced to play it all the way. He has the race to try out his products, but he must take the chance that they will fail. The fan may merely sit and watch, and buy his own parts on the strength of what happens on the tracks of the country, Indy being the major one.

When a new car appears, fans watch it with great interest. The new ideas on the car are studied in detail in the press. Perhaps a car is trying a different type of engine, or a radical new suspension system, or some other very obvious departure from the normal. Or, perhaps it is something not so obvious—fuel cells, a new brake system, or a tire rubber compound just developed. Whatever it might be, facts about the item or system are made known to the fans and they watch with interest.

If it works, it is almost certain that it will appear later on passenger cars. If it doesn't . . . well, hopefully it won't cost the life of a driver. In any case, it won't cost a fan his life.

Yet all of these important benefits are really only a side effect, important to engineers and car manufacturers primarily. Eventually they will become important to the fan, but his primary interest in the race is the great drama and speed and tradition of the event itself.

With the fan in mind, the Indianapolis Motor Speedway has been constantly improved over the years. The bricks disappeared under a new, faster, safer surface until only one yard of bricks, at the starting line, remains of the millions once in evidence. The old wooden stands were gradually replaced by concrete and steel grandstands of comfort and convenience. The old timing stands, replaced by the familiar "Pagoda," have been finally replaced by a glass and steel building at the starting line known as "Tower Terrace." The pits and garage area have been improved for safer operation and better fan visibility.

Some retaining walls were removed, and others built, to better protect fans from spinning race cars, and to help protect drivers by attempting to avoid head-on smashups on the track. Under the reign of track owner Tony Hulman, vast improvements of the grounds were made and continue to be made, turning the Indianapolis Motor Speedway into a beautiful, super-modern racing plant.

Today the race is no longer a smoky, difficult-to-see, tiring grind. It is a sleek, modern competition designed for the fan to enjoy, operated on a split-second schedule and according to iron-bound tradition. Today it is easier for over a quarter of a million fans to get in and get out than it once was for 50,000. Today, it is "the" automobile race in the world.

Here's how it works.

The first part of May the track is opened for practice. Until mid-April entries have been flowing into the track offices, and when the track opens these 80 or 90 cars, drivers and crews move into their assigned garages in Gasoline Alley. Long days and nights of preparation follow, aimed at the first of the four qualification days. Rookie drivers, in the meantime, are certified after stringent testing, and cars are certified after close examination by technical officials.

Finally qualification days begin, and one by one the cars may take to the track alone for four laps. The average speed over these four laps is the most important thing for the car and crew, for only the 33 fastest cars will be allowed to start the 500-mile race on Memorial Day. Once a car has qualified, that is it. Mechanics may tear it down and rebuild it, but the starting position stands.

On the final day of qualification after the last of the ready cars have run and the closing gun has been fired, the 33 are announced. The other 50-odd cars must wait until next year, in spite of the fact that many owners have invested more than $100,000 in the failing effort. And probably, to make the matter even worse for the owner, next year will mean newer and better cars in the field. His own will by then be out-dated.

On Memorial Day morning, as hundreds of thousands of fans stream into the stands, and as dozens of bands and celebrities parade around the track, the 33 chosen ones are lined up in the pit section. Then, as the time approaches for the start, they are pushed out onto the grid into position.

As drivers settle themselves into cockpits and are strapped in by crews, traditional music is played. "Taps" is sounded for the war dead, and "Back Home Again in Indiana" floats across the packed, hushed stands and infield. Bombs explode overhead periodically.

Then track owner Tony Hulman, standing in the rear seat of the passenger automobile which will pace the start of the race, gives his traditional command.

"Gentlemen, start your engines!!"

A staccato rumble fills the air as engine after engine fires and steadies into a deep, powerful idle. Then, as crews scurry over the wall for the safety of the pits, the pace car moves slowly away and the three fastest qualifiers, in the front row, creep along after it. The other thirty follow slowly, aligning themselves behind the front row.

Around the track they go in a long, colorful rectangle immediately behind the pace car. Flashing across the starting line the drivers wave as the crowd cheers. Around once more they go, increasing speed, until the pace car rockets out of the fourth turn and onto the long main straightaway at 100 miles per hour. Still the low-slung racers behind are loafing along.

But not for long.

For the pace car swerves to the left at the entrance to the pit section and screams past the empty stalls. At the same time the starter waves his green flag, and green lights snap on around the course. And the wildest, most thrilling, most nerve-wracking moment in all of sports begins.

Thirty-three of the finest drivers in the world guide 33 perfectly prepared racing machines into the first turn, increasing speed all the way, engines thundering and straining with unleashed power.

Another magnificent 500-mile race has begun . . . and nobody thinks of the automotive developments which will certainly result.

RIGHT One of the smallest, lightest cars to finish in the inaugural race at Indianapolis was this Mercer driven by Hughie Hughes, an early-day motor racing champion. Hughes chose to drive the Mercer even though it was underpowered with its small 300-cubic-inch engine. Hughes placed 12th in the race, winning less than $500, but he had the distinction of being the only small car entry to finish the grinding 500 miles.

BELOW Directly involved in the very first major crash at the Indianapolis Motor Speedway was this 546-cubic-inch Apperson, in the pits at the time. While driver Herbert Lytle and his mechanic were working on the car, a Case driven by Joe Jagersberger lurched on the main stretch on lap 87 and mechanic C. L. Anderson fell onto the track. Harry Knight's Westcott thundered onto the scene, swerved hard to miss the fallen Anderson, and plowed directly into Lytle's Apperson. Both Lytle and his mechanic were thrown through the air, into the next pit, but neither man was injured seriously, as were none of the others in the spectacular crash . . . though several spent time in a hospital with severe cuts and bruises.

◀ **PREVIOUS PAGE** This Case automobile, driven by Lewis Strang in the very first 500-mile race in 1911, was one of three identical cars entered. All three developed trouble with the steering gear. Very small cars with engines of only 284 cubic inches, the first Case went out in the violent crash on lap 87, this one dropped out on lap 109 and the final Case was sidelined on lap 122 with steering problems.

RIGHT Ray Harroun drove this 477-cubic-inch Marmon to victory in the first 500-mile race at the Indianapolis Motor Speedway. In a smooth, trouble-free race, Harroun took 6 hours, 42 minutes and 8 seconds to drive the distance, averaging 74.59 miles per hour. Harroun, who had announced his retirement from auto racing before the big race, came back to lead for more than 300 miles . . . though at no time was the field far behind. On this car Harroun, who drove without a riding mechanic, had mounted the wedge-shaped "world's first rear view mirror" so that he could see the cars coming up from the rear. A Marmon "Wasp," the six-cylinder car took the lead from David Bruce-Brown at the halfway point, and led all the rest of the way to the checkered flag.

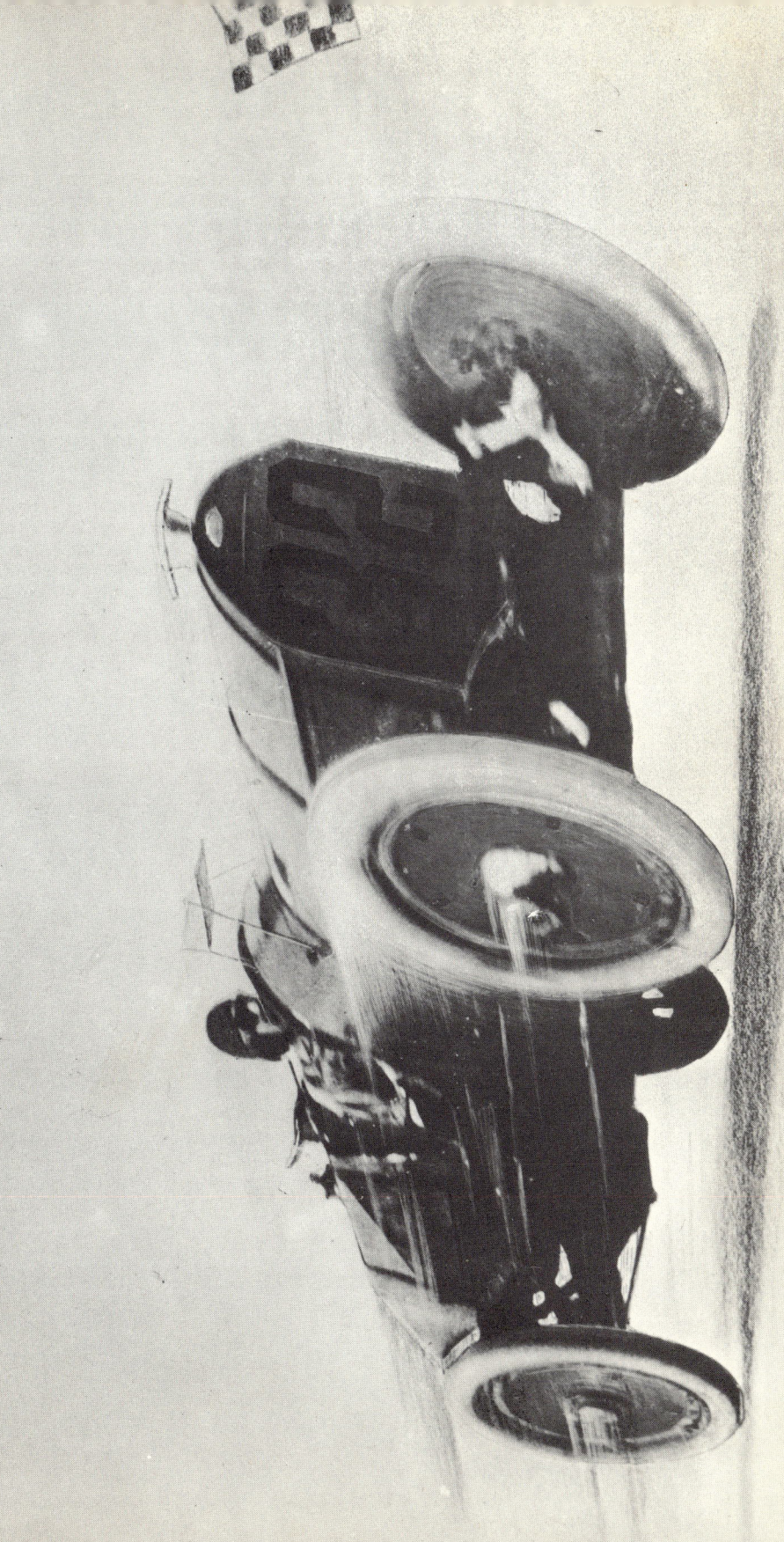

RIGHT One of two smaller displacement Cases in the 1912 race, this one was started last in the field of 24 by Louis Disbrow and his mechanic. Disbrow drove the six-cylinder racer until the 55th lap, when a team car driven by Neil Whalen dropped out with a broken camshaft bearing. Whalen then relieved Disbrow at the wheel of this car, but it too dropped out soon, shearing a differential pin on the 67th lap, to end the hopes of the Case contingent.

BELOW In a fancy new driving uniform, Ralph Mulford and his mechanic drove this new, highly streamlined Knox automobile to 10th place in the 1912 race. It was the way he did it that mattered, though. His first time in a Knox, Mulford encountered engine trouble on the 78th lap after running constantly with the leaders. One half hour of pit work corrected the problem, but by then the Knox was far behind. Returning to the track, Mulford drove on . . . and on . . . and on. Officials had flagged in the winner and the first nine cars (all that were running except for Mulford) but refused to allow him 10th place unless he finished. So, he did. He ran on for 8 hours and 53 minutes before empty stands and tired officials, until he finally finished the 500 miles, and won the $1200 for 10th place.

RIGHT Another bright red car which competed in the 1912 classic at Indianapolis was this Schacht, driven by Bill Endicott. Behind the scooping boilerplate nose was a four-cylinder engine of 389.9 cubic inches. Considering that the 1912 race was open to cars with engines of up to 600 cubic inches, and considering that several more powerful cars came in well behind Endicott, the team did very well when they placed fifth in the event. Note the steering wheel position of this Schacht. With the driver leaning out, as he did, it would be directly in front of him.

BELOW A striking car and crew in the 1912 race was this bright red Firestone-Columbus, driven by Lee Frayer, which started in the middle of the third five-car row. Frayer and his mechanic also wore bright red uniforms. The sleek and racy Columbus had worked its way up to sixth place at the end of 100 miles when it retired with intake valve problems.

RIGHT Harry Endicott's Nyborg was one of three six-cylinder cars entered in the 1913 event. The low-tailed car had an L-head engine with comparatively small valves (1 7/8 inches in diameter with a 3/8-inch lift) for a racing car. The car weighed 2300 pounds. It was Endicott's idea to point the nose and tail, and to flare the cowl in front of the wheel, to cut wind resistance. The engine was a 376.9-cubic-inch model (total displacement had been cut to 450 cubic inches for the first time this year). The car dropped out of the race on lap 23 when the reverse shaft in the gearbox seized.

BELOW The story of the 1912 race was written by this car and driver, though they did not win. The car was a Mercedes, a huge, heavy racer which weighed 2500 pounds. The driver, shown here winning the 1912 Vanderbilt Cup race in the same car, was the great Ralph DePalma. Quickly taking the lead from "Terrible Teddy" Tetzlaff at the beginning of the 1912 Indy race, DePalma was, at 250 miles, more than two laps ahead of his nearest rival. With 100 miles to go, the Mercedes was a full five laps ahead of Joe Dawson, running in second place. But then, on lap 195, the sound of power from the engine changed to a clanking clatter. One of the four connecting rods had broken and torn a hole in the crankcase. Oil poured from under the racer. DePalma tried to nurse the car along, but it finally came to a smoking stop on the backstretch on the 199th lap. Still unwilling to give up, DePalma and his riding mechanic, Rupert Jeffkins, started to push the car down the backstretch toward the third turn. At that moment, Joe Dawson, a hometown boy from Indianapolis, thundered by on his 197th lap. Unable to accept certain defeat, DePalma and Jeffkins kept pushing the heavy car, but as they struggled down the main straightaway to complete their 199th lap, Dawson swept under the checkered flag to win the 1912 classic. A thunderous ovation for Dawson soon turned to an even louder ovation for DePalma and Jeffkins as they staggered along, finally pushing the car into the pits. They had lost, but they and their car had joined the legendary cars and drivers of Indy.

RIGHT One of the sleekest cars in the 1913 race was Bob Burman's Keeton. Its meshwork hood and racing stripes caught the fancy of the fans. The reason for the meshwork was that the radiator was located behind the engine, a 448.72-cubic-inch T-head model with cylinders cast in pairs, two of two. Burman, a holder of several American speed records, and who was late arriving at the starting line, finally thundered into the lead in only 20 miles. He held this lead, stretching it to 3 minutes over eventual winner Jules Goux, till the 120-mile mark, when his carburetor caught fire and he was in the pits for a full hour. He finally returned to place 12th at the finish.

BELOW R. C. Liesaw's bent-looking racer for the 1913 race was called an Anel (which was Lena, backwards). The engine was a familiar four-cylinder valve-in-head model, but the car was unique in two respects. Rather than aluminum, the crankcase was made of bronze (to Liesaw's specs) and the car had no differential. Liesaw had worked his way up to ninth place when he was forced out of the race at 370 miles with loose connecting rods.

RIGHT Some unique streamlining ideas were evident in the 1913 race, among them the sharply pointed leading edges of nearly everything on this Mercedes-Knight. Driver and citizen of Belgium Theodore Pillete, an "amateur" driver of note and holder of several European speed records, combined the Mercedes automobile (he was a Mercedes dealer in Belgium) and the small Knight motor, and the combination worked. Although the Knight was a small four-cylinder engine of only 250 cubic inches (compared to engines of up to 449 cubic inches which finished behind the Knight) Pillete ran a race of remarkable consistency and moved up steadily to finally finish in fifth place with an average speed of 69.14 mph.

BELOW The bomb-shaped Mason of Willie Haupt was part of a three-car Mason team in the 1913 Indy classic. Shown here during a pit stop, the engine of the Mason was similar to the 1913 Duesenberg, with valves which extended horizontally into the side of the cylinder, and push rods and rocker arms working in and out rather than up and down. Haupt moved this number 35 Mason into second place in the race and had drawn to within 100 yards of leader Jules Goux, when time lost in the pits dropped him well back in the field. He eventually finished in ninth place. The single-seater Masons had a displacement of 350.50 cubic inches.

RIGHT One of America's foremost drivers in 1913 was Spencer Wishart, shown here in one of America's great hopes during the foreign-dominated 1913 event. Part of a three-car team, this Mercer boasted a T-head engine of 299.7 cubic inches with cast steel pistons and one of the world's first timing gears (most used timing chains). The new lighter Rudge-Whitworth wire wheels were being experimented with at this race. Wishart brought the relatively standard racing car from 16th to ninth place, when he was relieved by the great Ralph DePalma, another Mercer team driver whose car was out of the race. DePalma moved the car from ninth to third place, then Wishart jumped back in and moved up one more position. The car finished in second place with a speed of 73.49 mph.

BELOW One of the Frenchmen who soundly beat the Americans in the 1913 Indy classic was Albert Guyot, shown here in the car in which he did it, an English Sunbeam. The riding mechanic is R. F. L. Crossman. This Sunbeam racer, previously driven by Dario Resta to a 50-mile record of 92.96 miles per hour in England, had several unique features. The fore and aft pipes running down the side of the car were oil coolers. The oil was merely pumped the length of these pipes before going back through the engine. To save water which might be boiled away, a condenser was mounted atop the radiator cap. A long scooping nose helped to guide the air to cool the six-cylinder L-head engine of 367 cubic inches. Initially used on this Sunbeam in 1913, but now a standard item, were fins to help cool the brakes. The Guyot-driven car finished fourth.

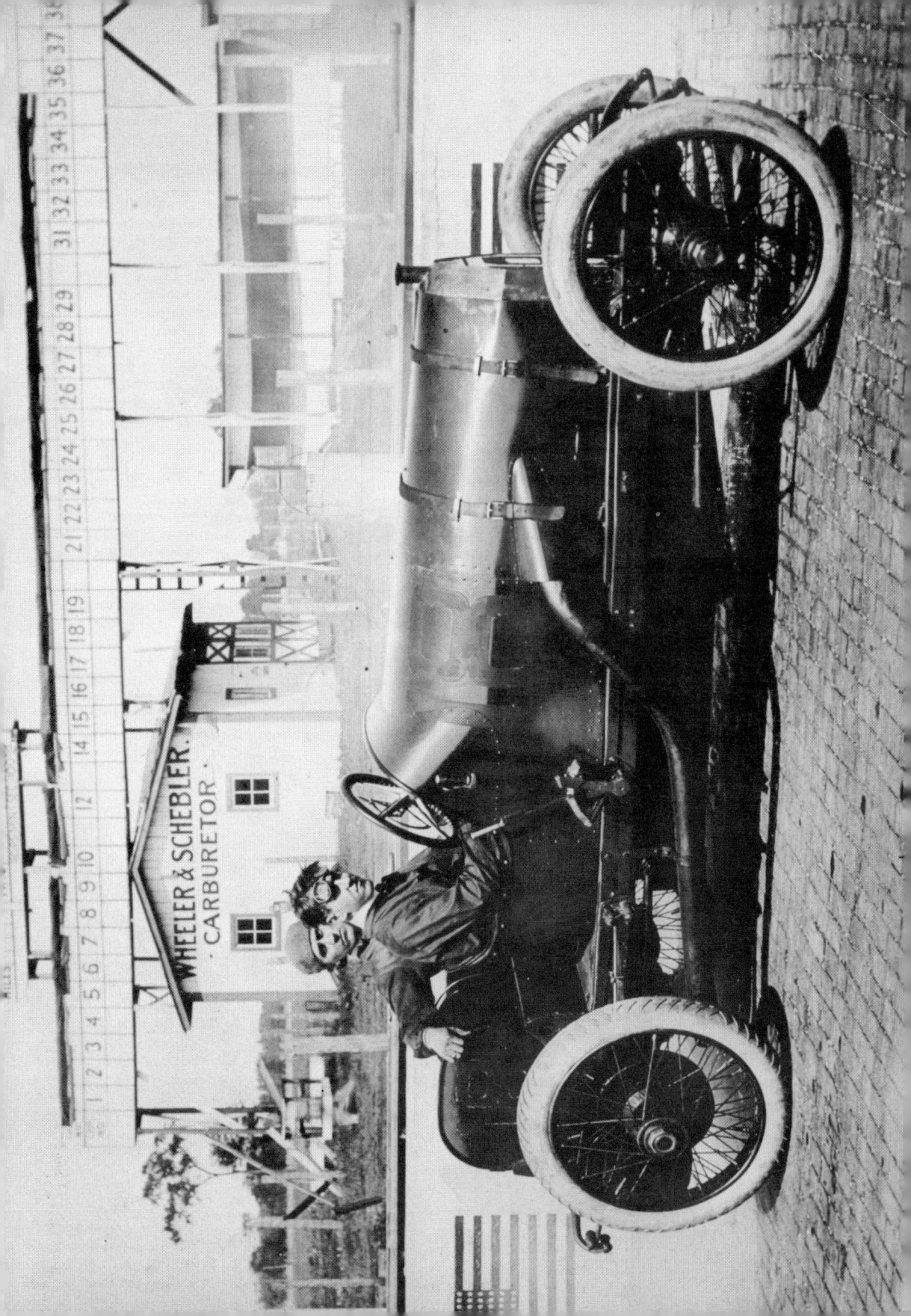

RIGHT Two famous names, Rickenbacker and Duesenberg, and one of the most exciting moments in the 1914 500-mile race, though Rickenbacker (shown here) had turned his car over to Willie Haupt temporarily. The engine of the "Duesie" was a four-cylinder model with 360.5-cubic-inch displacement. Note the open-end exhaust. It was felt that the inrush of air would help to carry away the exhaust gases. At the very end of the race Haupt, in this car, was leading Carlson's Maxwell for ninth place by three laps. But the Duesie needed a tire so, with plenty of time, Haupt pulled in for the change. Then the engine wouldn't start, and as one crewman after another frantically turned the crank until he fell exhausted to the ground, Carlson's Maxwell closed the gap. Just as somebody thought to jack up the rear, spin the tire, then push the car off the jack, starting it at last, the Maxwell swept by. Haupt could not catch Carlson in the laps remaining, and finished in 10th place.

BELOW America's hopes for the 1914 500-mile race centered on the three-car Stutz team, specifically on Barney Oldfield, shown here, who was back in good standing in AAA (after his fourth "lifetime suspension" for competing on outlaw tracks, and against animals and airplanes). A "secret" car at the time, the machine attracted reporters almost as strongly as the publicity conscious Oldfield. The Stutz was a four-cylinder, 296-cubic-inch entry. Though the lightweight wire wheels were proving quite popular, the Stutz team remained with the heavy-spoked wooden wheels. In the race Oldfield drove consistently from start to finish, averaging 79.14 mph. He was loudly cheered when he pulled into his pit after the finish, since he was the first American driver in an American car to finish this American classic. He took fifth place, behind Frenchmen Goux (fourth), Guyot (third), Duray (second) and Thomas, the winner.

RIGHT With the size of engines once again cut (to 300 cubic inches), Ralph DePalma, who had been having very bad luck at the Speedway, obtained a magnificent machine. It was one of the team cars of Mercedes, a team which had taken the first three places in the French Grand Prix in 1914. These cars had so shattered the confidence of French ace driver Boillot that he was finally led from his car, a Peugeot, crying like a baby. The Mercedes shown here became a classic racing and roadster design, and was used in modified forms until 1929. Overhead valves had been proven, spark plugs had improved tremendously, tires were much better than only two or three years before. Only two stops were required for each, as the 1915 race developed into a two-car battle between Dario Resta in a Peugeot and DePalma in the Mercedes. For lap after lap, DePalma would grab the lead in the turns, and Resta would take it back along the straightaways. On his final laps, just as happened in 1912, DePalma felt the car lurch as a connecting rod let go inside the engine... but this time he was able to get the car to the finish line where he took the checkered flag as the winner with an average speed, a great new record, of 89.84 miles per hour.

BELOW Albert Guyot steers his powerful Delage racer around the outside of the track in 1914. Identical to the winning Delage, this car placed third with Guyot at the wheel, though it had led part of the way. Between the two huge Delages, which were super-powered racers of 380.2 cubic inches and with bore and stroke measurements of 4.1 and **seven** inches, came a little 183-cubic-inch Peugeot driven by Leon Duray into second place. Guyot's teammate, René Thomas, won the race. Guyot won slightly over $5000 for his efforts, though third place now pays more than ten times that amount. A new record speed for the race was set by the winner at 82.47 miles per hour, as the old racers became more efficient and reliable.

RIGHT As they became more and more reliable, racing cars seemed to be appearing more delicate, less square and boxy. This 1916 Crawford, driven in the race by Chandler, was light but strong. Under the hood was a 298-cubic-inch engine which just nudged the 300-cubic-inch limit. Part of a three-car team, and one of the few new cars of 1916 (the Speedway was suffering from lack of entries due to the war scare) this one finally placed ninth in the Indy "300" (it was shortened this year, and then stopped altogether during the First World War). The Speedway owned three Premiers, two Peugeots and a Maxwell, just to help fill the field.

BELOW This Stutz, driven by Earl Cooper (shown here at the wheel) was one of a two-car team for the 1915 race. The car was the same as the one driven by Barney Oldfield in 1914, but with the newer, now proven wire wheels. Remarkably, but an indication of the solidarity of these machines with each passing year, the hoods were not raised on either Stutz throughout the entire 500-mile race, and this one with Cooper at the wheel, placed fourth, while teammate Anderson placed third.

RIGHT When the 500-mile race resumed after World War I, to prophecies that auto racing would never regain its former stature, the stands at Indy were packed. But the race was not without tragedy. Three men died. Two of them are shown here, marking them as the first men to have died during a 500-mile race at Indy since 1911. This Roamer, one of two such cars in the race, was driven by Louis LeCocq. Entered by racing great Roscoe Sarles, the 299-cubic-inch Duesenberg-powered car hurtled into its 97th lap when, just in front of Grandstand G, the gas tank suddenly exploded in a ball of flame. Instantly the car flipped over, pinning both driver and mechanic underneath. LeCocq and mechanic Robert Bandini, shown here with LeCocq, were burned to death in the terrible accident.

BELOW The sharp, pointed tail on this fine old racer helped fans identify the English-built Sunbeam during the 1916 race at Indianapolis. Driven by Josef Christiaens, the car was one of very few given a chance to beat the heavily favored Dario Resta. The engine was a typical six-cylinder Sunbeam of 299 cubic inches. Larger and heavier than most of the cars in the race, the Sunbeam was also reliable. Eddie Rickenbacker led the race for a few laps at first in one of the Speedway's cars (the Maxwell) but, as expected, Resta took the lead and went on to win the 300-mile event. Christiaens placed fourth.

RIGHT Another consistent performer in the 1919 race was Tom Alley in the four-cylinder Bender racer. Many sportswriters of the day pointed out the smooth drive of this Ahlberg Bearing Company entry. Alley's ride was particularly notable in view of the high attrition rate of the field. Only thirteen cars were running at the finish, some of these far behind. Thirty-three had started the race. Three men were killed during accidents. Alley completed the race in six hours, five minutes, to take fifth place.

BELOW Ira Vail, in this Hudson race car, was one of the most consistent runners in the first post-war 500-mile race. The six-cylinder, 288-cubic-inch Hudson motor performed flawlessly while other cars were dropping out steadily. Vail brought the Hudson in to finish in eighth place in the 1919 classic.

RIGHT When, though, would an American car, driven by an American driver, win the great race at Indy again. Not since 1912 had this happened, and fans were ready for it. Veteran racing driver Louis Chevrolet considered the new size restrictions of 183 cubic inches, and designed and built his own car, which he called a Monroe. His brother Gaston drove it in the 1920 "500." The engine was a four-cylinder model of 182.5 cubic inches and the body was specifically designed for Indy. Meanwhile, accessory companies were in-fighting and improving their equipment because of it, to get their products on Indy cars. Goodyear and Goodrich and Firestone were competing. In spark plugs, Champion and AC were challenging KLG for supremacy, and several other accessory companies were in the scramble. To the great delight of over 120,000 fans, Gaston Chevrolet drove a careful race and moved into the lead near the end. He won the 1920 race with a speed of 88.16 miles per hour, as the remaining cars in the Chevrolet team were dropping out with failing steering arms. Later, as Gaston and Louis were congratulating themselves over the huge amount of money they had won, Louis complained that it would be even more if the steering arms hadn't broken. So saying, he nudged the arm on Gaston's car . . . and it snapped off too. But it had held as you see it here, on the bricks of Indy.

BELOW One of the great drivers of the day was Howard "Howdy" Wilcox, shown here in a Speedway-owned Peugeot in which he drove in the 1919 "500." The Peugeot, originally a French car, had been Americanized by the addition, one by one, of American parts as the foreign parts broke or wore out. Behind the Packard V12 pace car the field thundered away on time, with DePalma and Louis Chevrolet fighting for the lead for the entire first half of the race. But then Wilcox, who had been cruising along smoothly, took over. He won the 1919 race at a speed of 87.95 miles per hour.

RIGHT This magnificent machine was started in the 1921 race by Eddie Miller, and finished by Jimmy Murphy. The racer is a classic Duesenberg Straight-8, a car and engine upon which many, many others were modeled during these grand days of automobile experimentation and improvement. Clean and simple in its lines, the "Duesie" helped to begin the straight eight revolution (in fact, the 1921 winning car had a straight eight engine partially copied directly from Duesenberg plans). In a sense the Offenhausers of its day, there were seven of these fine machines entered in 1921. Four of them finished in the top 10, a fine example of speed and reliability. This one, with Murphy at the wheel near the end, finished fourth.

BELOW One of the most formidable teams in the 1921 500-mile race included this sleek Sunbeam-powered Talbot-Darracq, driven by Andre Boillot. Most of the racers of this year were equipped to keep too much heat from collecting under the hood, but these Sunbeams **really** did the job with their huge right side scoop. The added sheet metal in front of the driver deflected the wind over his head, but as usual, the mechanic got the wind full in his face. The three-car team, as formidable as it might have appeared, did not do well, Ora Haibe brought an identical Talbot-Darracq into fifth place, but the others dropped out . . . this one with a burned-out connecting rod bearing on the 41st lap.

RIGHT By 1923 the rule that all cars had to have a riding mechanic was dropped, and every racer in the 1923 Indy event was a single seater. Also, once again, the size of engines was reduced with the maximum displacement now 122 cubic inches. This didn't bother the fans, though, since the smaller, more modern engines were consistently beating the times of the older, larger ones. But it did bother the drivers, for the new light cars bounced about on the track like bucking horses . . . until almost immediately a better spring and shock arrangement was developed. Also, for the first time in 1923, certain of the top stars, including Milton, Murphy, Wilcox and Hartz, used a brand new gasoline additive developed by Charles Kettering, and known as "Ethyl." Prince de Cystria, shown here in his 1923 Bugatti, with an eight-cylinder, 121-cubic-inch engine, suffered handling problems throughout the race, but finally managed to out-last many others and finish in ninth place.

BELOW Although the Duesenberg brothers made a nearly clean sweep of the first 10 places in the 1922 500-mile race at Indy, they did not come in as winners. San Francisco's Jimmy Murphy, riding with mechanic Ernie Alson, both men fresh from their victory in the 1921 French Grand Prix, led the race for a total of 154 laps and won by a two-lap margin over rookie Harry Hartz. At that, Duesenberg was represented, for the chassis of Murphy's car was a Duesenberg. Murphy, however, had removed the engine and installed a 181-cubic-inch eight-cylinder Miller, and this proved to be the proper combination. The only non-Duesenbergs in the first 10 were Eddie Hearne's Ballot (third) and Tom Alley's Monroe (ninth).

PREVIOUS PAGE But the man with real problems in the 1923 race was the German Karl Sailer, driving this Mercedes four-cylinder model. First, the tail of his car caught fire in the pits as a backfire from the engine ignited spilled fuel. Sailer quickly exited his car until the fire was put out. Second, the general pit work of the Sailer team, and the entire German contingent of three Mercedes, was sloppy and uncoordinated. The Germans were unaccustomed to, and amazed by, the precision pit work of the Americans, who could entirely service a car much quicker than they could add fuel. Finally, Sailer and his team drivers could not handle the track as well as the other competitors. They would skid at the wrong places, accelerate where they should have been slowing down, and vice versa. Of the three cars, however, two finished the race, with Sailer taking a creditable eighth place with a final average speed of 80.68 miles per hour (compared to winner Milton's 90.95 miles per hour).

RIGHT Earl Cooper, one of the all time high drivers in point standings, fought a bitter battle for victory in the 1924 race, but he was out-gunned by America's first development and use of a supercharger. Cooper's Studebaker Special, a standard eight-cylinder machine modified for racing by the Studebaker Company, was fast and with its chrome radiator and downward discharging exhausts quite racy. It was one of the favorites to win and indeed was battling for the lead in mid-race with Jimmy Murphy in a Miller Special. But up from the rear, driving relief for L. L. Corum, came a screaming Joe Boyer in a supercharged Duesenberg. In the final 55 miles of the 1924 race, fans witnessed one of the most spectacular duels in racing history, the battle between Cooper and Boyer. Finally, however, the extra power of the supercharged Duesie carried Boyer a few seconds ahead at the finish.

RIGHT Peter DePaolo, nephew and ex-riding mechanic of the great Ralph DePalma, wanted to become a driver. He was given a chance, finally, and he proved to be like his uncle, a natural born racing driver. He never again worked as a mechanic, and finally he became the first driver in history to average over 100 miles per hour for the 500-mile race at Indy, a race he won in the car shown here. This car is an eight-cylinder, 121.780-cubic-inch Duesenberg, supercharged, as was the Duesie which won the year before. DePaolo averaged 101.19 miles per hour to win the 1925 event, after beating back a challenge by Bennett Hill in the Miller Junior 8 (called the car of the future because of its front-wheel-drive system).

BELOW The real pioneer in a long string of cars reaching all the way to today (and through many, many military and commercial vehicles as well as modern road vehicles) appeared in the 1925 race and did quite well, leading for a part of the way. This was the little light blue 121-cubic-inch Junior 8, a Miller-engined car driven by Dave Lewis. The car appeared much smaller than the others in the race, and was distinctive due to the odd bulge in the front axle. The bulge covered the front-wheel-drive mechanism developed by Miller and eventually became quite popular in racing and stock use. Lewis led the race after eventual winner Pete DePaolo was forced to pit at the halfway mark, but on lap 173 Lewis came in for relief and DePaolo went on to win. The car finally placed second with Lewis again at the wheel, one half lap behind the winner.

RIGHT Other racers were not yet ready for 500 grinding miles. Take this Locomobile Special entered by Cliff Durant. A typical Miller-type eight-cylinder engine with a displacement of 90.2 cubic inches to meet the new 91.5 limit powered the car, but it met with little success in the race. Supercharged, and with every indication that it might go all the way at the beginning, the car soon began to make lengthy pit stops for a wide variety of problems, including gas tank leaks, carburetor adjustments, tire changes, water and gas and oil additions, shock absorber adjustments and even pressure adjustments in the tires. Durant finally dropped out for good with a serious gas leak.

BELOW On the pole position for the 1926 race was Earl Cooper in a car which had become the topic of conversation among racing fans, one of the Miller front-drive specials. Similar in general appearance to the first such cars of the year before, the '26 Miller front-drive models had a new engine to meet the new size restrictions of 91.5 cubic inches or under. The front axles were built in three tubular sections, bolted together, with the center section easily removable for access to the transmission, without disturbing the axle as a whole. Unfortunately, Cooper pitted almost immediately after the race started, and this began a long series of pit stops which put him well back in the field when the race was stopped for the first time due to rain. The Miller wouldn't start at the re-start, though it finally did reenter the race momentarily before dropping out for good with a broken gear.

RIGHT For the very first time appearing like a "modern" race car (though the sheet metal work of today is far more lovingly detailed) this Eldridge Special, driven by W. D. Hawkes, almost lived in the pits. While Miller Specials were placing first, second, third, fourth, sixth, seventh, eighth, ninth and tenth, that's all but DePalolo's Duesie which placed fifth, Hawkes was worrying over his four-cylinder (with rollers at every main and con rod bearing) engine. On winner Lockhart's 122nd lap, Hawkes was on his 83rd. After a grand total of 12 pit stops, the sleek-looking racer finally pulled in permanently with a frozen camshaft, as rookie Lockhart took the 1926 checkered flag.

BELOW Lora L. Corum's Schmidt Special was one of two such cars in the 1926 500-mile race. By 1926 all cars, including the Schmidts, were supercharged and all cars used the now-proven balloon tires, wire wheels and modern shock absorbers. Hydraulic brakes were on most cars. The Schmidt Specials (as well as the Guyot Special) had engines with a special type of single sleeve, an experimentation of Continental Motors Corp. In an effort to more quickly scavenge exhaust gases, the company had even drilled extra ports in the sleeves which were cleared when the piston reached the bottom of the stroke. It didn't work though. The piston rings caught on the edges of the ports and broke. In fact, nothing else seemed to work either, and L. L. dropped out of the race finally with a cracked engine block.

RIGHT Without question one of the brightest cars ever to run at Indy was this Chromolite Special, driven by Earl DeVore in 1928. Every bit of metal was chromium plated, making the car gleam beautifully. During this period of supercharging, one of the problems faced by race car builders and mechanics was to discover a method of cooling down the hot fuel from the supercharger before it entered the cylinders. Most cars used an air-cooled "intercooler"... but not the Chromolite Special. This car had a special radiator which surrounded the regular engine radiator, for cooling the water used in the liquid-cooled intercooler. Did it work? Yes, until DeVore rammed the wall in the southwest turn on the 162nd lap and destroyed the handsome race car.

BELOW More improvements in automobiles, all reflected in this Erskine Miller front-wheel-drive of Harry Hartz, came in the 1927 race. Inverted carburetors were giving better engine performance, high pressure blowers were giving more power, new inlet manifolds were giving better reliability and lower centers of gravity were giving better control and safety. Each year now, like a man stumbling forward faster and faster, cars were being altered and changed and modified. Sometimes an idea worked, and was passed on to street machines... other times it didn't, and perhaps a racing driver died. Unfortunately for Harry Hartz, a universal joint failed in his Miller, and the National Champion was out of the race on lap 38.

RIGHT The last year for the 91.5-cubic-inch displacement limit was 1929, and one of the cars checking in under this limit was this French Delage Special, driven by Louis Chiron. The car was small, light and built very low to the ground . . . too low, some said, "tending to skid rather than to tip in the turns." The engine was mounted with a Roots blower placed at the front, and valves were operated by two overhead camshafts. This car finished seventh, with Ray Keech winning the 1929 race in a Miller Special.

BELOW The prerace favorite of the 1928 "500" was easily Leon Duray in the Miller Special #4. This front-drive car was the holder of the new track record speed, 124.018 for one lap and 122.391 for four laps. And as predicted, Leon thundered away from the field and set a blistering pace for 64 laps but then he quickly began to fade to the rear. He finally pulled into the pits for the last time, with an overheated and frozen engine, on lap 134. Going on to win this 1928 race was Lou Meyer. Though no fan, of course, realized it then, Lou Meyer's name would be blazed into the history books forever, for he would eventually win two more races to become one of only four three-time winners to date.

RIGHT Powered by an unusual engine, Lou Meyer did very well in the 1925 Indy "500"—especially in view of the fact that "odd" cars rarely even finish the race. But Alden Sampson II, who served as builder and riding mechanic, looked at the record being compiled in racing by the Miller engines. Sampson, who also owned the car, then decided to take two such Miller engines and gear them together side-by-side, forming a 16-cylinder 201-cubic-inch powerplant. The snow-white car, with Meyer and Sampson in the cockpit, finished a solid fourth.

BELOW New huge engines appeared at Indy in 1930 with the new 366-cubic-inch limit, among them this "Romthe" Special, driven by J. C. McDonald and owned by the man who served as riding mechanic, William Richards. A Studebaker eight-cylinder President engine of 336 cubic inches powered the 2600-pound car. Billy Arnold took the lead on the third lap and went all the way to win the 1930 Indy race in his Miller-Hartz front-drive racer. This well-built (and well cared for) Romthe did well enough for 112 laps before it dropped out with a gas tank leak.

RIGHT Another of the semi-stocks in the 1931 event was this Buick-powered car of Red Shafer. Powered by an eight-cylinder Buick 60 engine, the car finished the race in 12th place with an average speed of 86.391 miles per hour. Manufacturers such as Buick learned a great deal about the performance and reliability of their products during the grueling 500 miles of Indy. They then passed this knowledge on to passenger units.

BELOW Dave Evans drove this four-cylinder diesel-powered racer in the 1931 Indy "500," and he didn't do badly. The 3400-pound car was one of several semi-stock cars in the field that year, a year which saw many, many crashes and injuries. Evans finished the race in the Cummins car, placing 13th at the end, and became the first car in history to go the entire 500 miles without a stop.

RIGHT By the 40th lap of the 1931 500-mile race, Louie Schneider had moved this non-stock Bowes Seal Fast Special, powered by an eight-cylinder Miller engine, into ninth place. From that point on it was a matter of moving up gradually, place by place until, on the 167th lap, with the elimination of Billy Arnold and Tony Gulotta in an accident, Schneider swept into the lead. He was not headed again and he took the checkered flag with an average speed of 96.629 miles per hour.

BELOW Yet another of the semi-stocks in the 1931 event was this huge old Reo Royale, racing as the Elco Royale Special. The car was powered by an eight-cylinder Reo engine, and placed ninth in the race with an average speed of 91.839 miles per hour. Nor would this be the last time the driver would be heard from, for driver Cliff Bergere went on through many races to become an all-time competitor at Indy. Some of his mileage records are still standing.

RIGHT Dave Evans was back in a Cummins Diesel in 1934, but it was a more powerful model. It had a four-cycle motor with a supercharger (Stubby Stubblefield's Cummins Diesel had a two-cycle motor). This car qualified at 102.414 (the winner's qualifying speed was 116.116 mph) and finally dropped out on lap 81 with mechanical problems.

BELOW The effects of full streamlining were beginning to show up in racing cars by 1932. This Gilmore Special, a 220.3-cubic-inch Miller-powered car, was taken to Muroc Dry Lake in Utah for closely controlled speed tests. Stubby Stubblefield was the driver on these tests, and at the "500." With a standard body on the car, top speed was found to be 137 miles per hour, but with this radically streamlined body and tail, top speed actually jumped to 148 miles per hour. The car finally finished the 1932 "500" in 16th place.

RIGHT By 1935 there were nine front-wheel-drive cars in the field. All four of Harry Miller's entries were front drives, and all four of them were powered by eight-cylinder, 220-cubic-inch Ford engines. One, shown here, was driven by the great Ted Horn, and serviced by riding mechanic Bo Huckman (of nearly equal fame). However, of 10 such cars built by Miller for Ford, and considered to be revolutionary in concept, even the four which made the field were unable to finish the race. Steering was the problem, and once again the "proving ground" at Indy provided further development along these lines. In all 10 cars, and in the four which made the race, the steering assembly was placed too near the engine block. The resulting heat caused the gears inside the steering assembly to expand and bind up. One by one, with the final one (shown here) going out on lap 145, the cars' front wheels locked up and could not be steered. Miller redesigned the steering after this race.

BELOW Kelly Petillo had his problems with this Gilmore Special, a four-cylinder Miller-powered racer, at least during qualifications. The first time out he ran out of gas, the second time he tore up his engine. On this third attempt, with a patched-up block, he finally qualified in mid-field. After a hot battle with Rex Mays, Petillo took the lead and held it to the end, in spite of a last-second charge by Wilbur Shaw, to become the 1935 Indy winner.

RIGHT Though it was not finished in time to qualify for the 1937 Indy classic, this car was one of the most interesting in Gasoline Alley. To be driven by Lee Oldfield, the car was powered by a massive 16-cylinder Marmon engine mounted in the rear. Another feature of this car was the fact that each wheel was independently sprung. There were many, many fans, and quite a few drivers too, who were disappointed when this futuristic car never took to the track for a qualification run.

BELOW Driver Frank McGurk and mechanic Karl Hattel qualified for the 1936 Indy race in this Abels Auto Ford Special. The car was very reminiscent of the earlier Miller-Gilmore Specials, but this one was powered by a Cragar-Ford four-cylinder engine. A beautiful racing car to see, the machine did not do well in the race, finally dropping out on lap 51 with a broken crankshaft. It was placed 26 in the order of finish.

RIGHT New fuel regulations were of no concern to Wilbur Shaw, who had finished second at Indy for two years in a row. This year he lavished every bit of his skill and love into this car which he designed and built himself. For an engine he chose the relatively new Offenhauser and for tires, of course, Firestone. The car was sponsored by a gasoline company, and the engine worked just fine on Gilmore gas. In fact, Shaw and mechanic Jigger Johnson were far ahead of second-place Ralph Hepburn near the end of the race. He appeared to be a certain winner of the 1937 "500." But then the trouble developed. Low on oil, Shaw was forced to slow down to save his engine (although he had time for a stop, regulations prohibited adding oil). Gradually Hepburn closed the gap until, on the very last lap, he actually nosed ahead of Shaw's car. Pushing his accelerator to the floor for the first time in 30 minutes, Shaw forced his car to speed faster and faster down the long straightaway. He beat Hepburn to the line by a scant 2.16 seconds for the closest finish in Speedway history.

BELOW One of the problems faced by this Maserati in 1937, and the Alfa Romeo of Rex Mays, was the new ruling on gasoline for the Indy classic. No longer would special racing fuels be allowed. All cars would run on a standard grade of gasoline. Mays' car and this one, driven by Babe Stapp, were built to run on alcohol, and so considerable modifications had to be made, including changing compression ratios and valve timing. When all modifications were finished, the foreign cars just weren't as fast as the Millers or the Offies. This one dropped out on the 36th lap, with clutch trouble the official reason.

RIGHT Harry McQuinn's 1938 Marchese Special was equipped with a frame made of aircraft tubing and was fitted with a radiator mounted outside the hood, to the lower left of the driver. This allowed an enclosed, streamlined nose. The car was suspended on special transverse springs. It was powered with an eight-cylinder Miller engine, and qualified at an average speed of 119.492 miles per hour for the '38 classic. Only five racers completed the full 500 miles in 1938, with this Marchese Special being withdrawn on lap 197. This was good enough to win seventh place for driver McQuinn.

BELOW Tony Gulotta in his sleek Burd Piston Ring Special, another Offenhauser-powered car in the 1937 Indy race, with mechanic John Pawl. This car finished the race in eighth place at an average speed of 105.015 miles per hour.

RIGHT This rear-engined car was designed by Harry Miller and driven by George Bailey in the 1939 Indianapolis 500-mile race. Incorporating several new features never before seen in championship racing, the car was powered by a six-cylinder supercharged engine (Miller) mounted in the rear, with the flywheel toward the front of the car. Drive was to all four wheels which were independently sprung on transverse springs. However, on lap 47 the car was withdrawn from the race with valve trouble and it did not return. This car was one of the heaviest in the race at 2102 pounds.

BELOW Ronney Householder is shown here in the Sparks-Thorne Special, powered by a six-cylinder Sparks engine with a centrifugal supercharger. The supercharger was most unique, being placed at the rear end of the engine and then driven from the gear train at the front end by means of a long solid shaft. The supercharger outlet was connected to the intake manifold by a hose coupling, tested before the race at 250 pounds pressure and thought to be adequate. This hose connection however cost both Householder, and Jimmy Snyder's identical car #6, the race when it blew out, forcing both cars out. Snyder's car dropped out on lap 150, and Householder's car moments later on lap 154.

PREVIOUS PAGE One of the most famous cars ever to run at Indianapolis was this sleek black Maserati, the Boyle Special. Ordered from its European factory by Boyle for Wilbur Shaw to race at Indy, the car was a precise handling machine of great beauty and speed. Shaw was so sure he would win in this car that he made a deal with his car owner that he would either win the 1939 race, or he would not receive one cent of pay. This was typical of Wilbur Shaw, who was cocky, confident, and who knew his racing cars. Shaw dominated the race in his eight-cylinder Italian car, putting down challenges by Lou Meyer (who retired after a crash in this race) and Chet Miller along the way. The race average speed, however, was well below what might have been expected due to a long caution period after a violent crash between Bob Swanson, Chet Miller and '38 winner Floyd Roberts, who was killed. Shaw won the race at a speed of 155.035 miles per hour.

RIGHT A great driver, and the very first appearance of a great car. Though this would be the last race until after the Second World War, this car would return to blaze a historic name in auto racing. Known in 1941 as the Bowes Seal Fast Special, the car was powered by a brand new supercharged V8 engine with overhead camshafts and a piston displacement of 183 cubic inches. The engine was designed by Ed Winfield and was said to produce 450 horsepower at 8000 rpm. The three carburetors were designed by Ed's brother, Bud Winfield, to keep the entire matter in the family. The car introduced to racing fans a new "howling" sound from its engine, a sound which would thrill fans for years to come. In 1941, Ralph Hepburn drove the car to a fourth-place finish as Mauri Rose relieved Floyd Davis and went on to win the first of his three "500s." Since the car was designed and built in a little town in Michigan, it became known by the same name . . . NOVI.

RIGHT Out on lap 25 of the 1946 race was this sleek Bowes Seal Fast Special driven by National Champion Rex Mays. The car dropped out with a broken manifold after being considered a leading threat to win the 500-mile race. Mays was awarded 30th place in the race.

BELOW When the 500-mile race resumed in 1946, several new cars appeared on the grid. Notable among them was this Fageol Twin Coach Special driven by Paul Russo. In an effort at effective weight distribution, proper center of gravity and constant tractive effort, this car was built with an engine at each end. The engines were not linked but drove independently of each other. Only a common throttle gave them identical speeds, each driving a pair of wheels. Powerplants were 91-cubic-inch Offenhauser engines, each boosted by a Rootes type blower. The car crashed on lap 17, and was out of the race.

RIGHT English driver R. M. W. Arbuthnot brought this pretty little semi-stock Lagonda all the way from England to compete in the Indianapolis "500," but the car was damaged en route to the Speedway and could not be repaired in time to qualify. Note the wrinkled rear end.

BELOW The first car on the track for practice after the several year shutdown was George Barringer's Tucker Torpedo Special, sponsored by one of the radical new car companies of the day. However, the bulky-looking rear-engined car, powered by a Tucker engine similar to that in the Tucker passenger car, suffered gear problems after only 26 laps of the race and dropped out. The Tucker Automobile Company eventually suffered the same fate, "dropping out" after only a few models were produced.

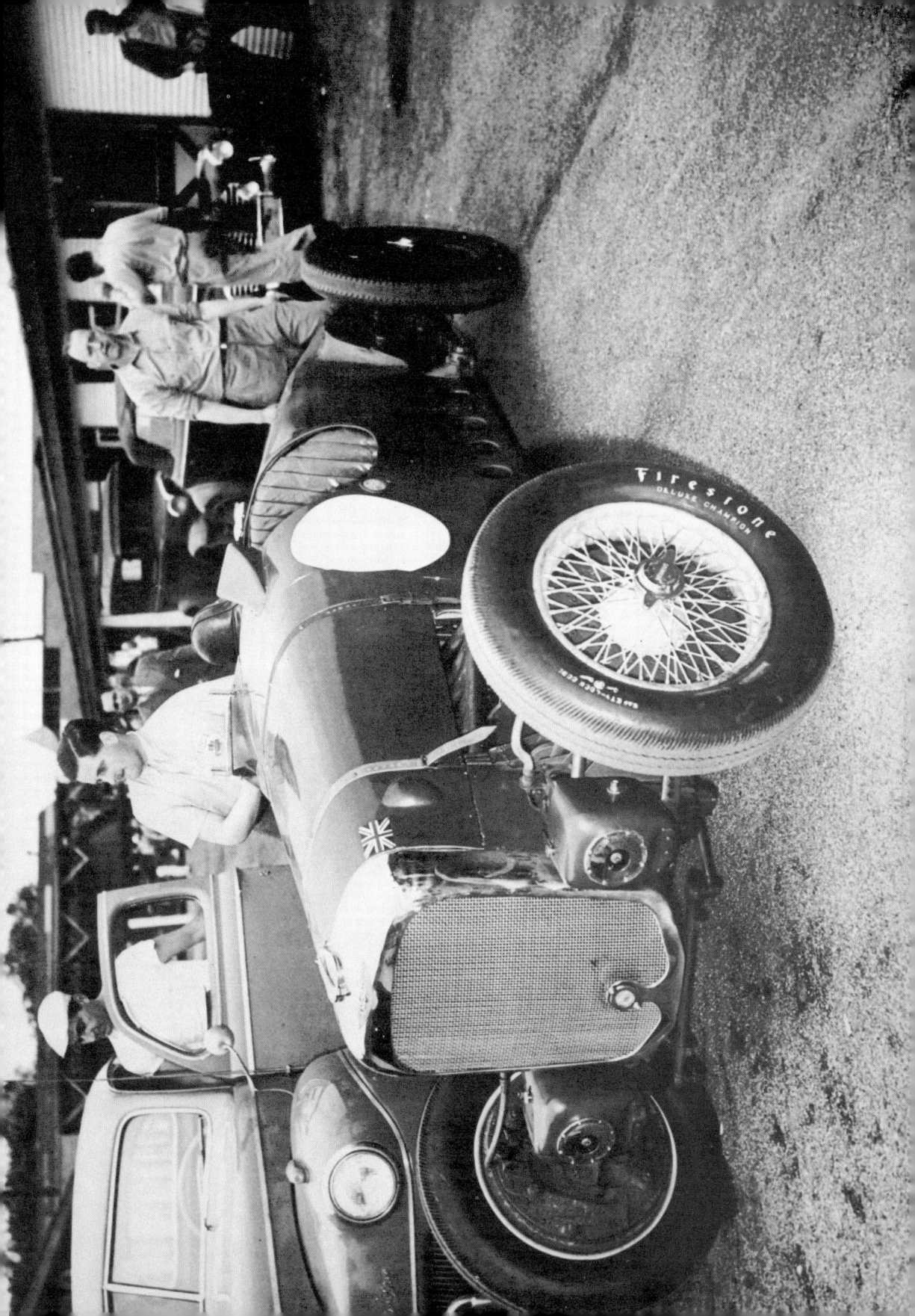

RIGHT The fastest car ever to run at the Speedway up to this time was the Novi Governor Special, which turned a blistering (for 1946) lap of 134.449 miles per hour under the hands of veteran Ralph Hepburn. With an engine based upon the V8 design of the 1941 Hepburn Novi, and with a brand new long, low, sleek body, the car attracted attention throughout the month of May. It could not be mistaken on the track, for the sound from its howling supercharger made your hair stand on end. Many fans said the car was overpowered and unsafe, a mankiller, but every fan watched it perform with great fascination. Hepburn was forced out of the 1946 race with engine trouble after 121 laps. In 1948 (after missing the 1947 event) in this car (then known as the Novi Grooved Piston Special) Hepburn was killed during practice.

BELOW The first of a long line of Blue Crown Spark Plug Specials was this 1946 Offy-powered racer of Mauri Rose. Unfortunately, Mauri crashed this car violently out of the '46 race on the 40th lap. Although Rose was not hurt badly, the car was destroyed.

RIGHT Cliff Bergere in the Novi in which Ralph Hepburn set a track record the year before, 1946. Due to certain driving conflicts Hepburn could not drive in 1947, so veteran Cliff Bergere stepped in to drive the wicked Novi. During practice for the race, Bergere spun out in the south turn and landed in a ditch full of water . . . leaving the white mark of repair on the nose of the Novi. During the race, the Novi stalled on lap 63 with engine problems, and was out of the race. Bergere, however, then relieved driver Herb Ardinger in an identical Novi and brought that car home in fourth place.

BELOW Pete Romcevich is shown here in the Andy Granatelli Ford V8 entry which Danny Kladis drove the year before (1946). This car was an almost stock Ford V8, front drive, and originally built by Harry Miller for the Ford Motor Company. In the 1946 race a mistake with a fuel shut-off switch caused the car to stall, and a push by a tow truck disqualified it. It had been doing well in the race until then. Kladis drove the car faster than any flathead had ever been driven at Indy. Known in 1947 as the Camco Special, the car was qualified by Romcevich into the middle of the sixth row for the start. The car finished in 12th place in the '47 500-mile race.

The beautiful twin Blue Crown Spark Plug Specials which dominated the 1947 race under the hands of Mauri Rose (right) and Bill Holland (below) . . . and which were responsible for one of the most controversial finishes ever at the Indy "500." These cars, identical, were designed and built by Lou Moore. They were front-wheel-drive models, powered by Offenhauser 270-cubic-inch four-cylinder engines of 4-5/16-inch bore and 4⅝-inch stroke. Total weight of the cars, not including fuel and oil, was approximately 1650 pounds, and top speed was estimated to be 170 miles per hour. Holland, a rookie at the Speedway, dominated the race, with Rose remaining always within striking distance. Near the end of the race, Rose began to close the gap . . . and Lou Moore couldn't get him to slow down. Moore didn't want an all-out battle between his two cars, but he could do little more than watch from the pits. Finally Rose streaked around Holland, who gave Mauri a casual wave, and so the race ended. Holland thought he was still more than a lap ahead, and it was with great disappointment that he learned he had placed second in the big race.

RIGHT Full-blooded Indian Joie Chitwood, thrill-show driver as well as racing driver and very popular among the fans, drove this Nyquist Special in the 1948 "500" at Indianapolis. Chitwood qualified the car very handily into the fourth row of starters with a speed of 124.619 miles per hour. Chitwood was doing well enough in the race (though every car was once again being overshadowed by the twin Blue Crown Specials of Rose and Holland) until the 98th lap, when a leak in his fuel tank developed and he was forced out.

BELOW Mr. STP himself, Andy Granatelli, in his 1948 Speedway entry. This Mercury-powered racer was personally designed and built by the Granatelli brothers. After nearly a full month of practice and tuning, Andy finally pronounced the car ready for qualification runs. As Granatelli pulled onto the track for his qualification run, the announcer mentioned that the car had already run 500 miles in practice. Andy's first three laps were completed at better than 123 miles per hour, and he was "in." All he had to do was finish his final lap but, as he started his last lap, the announcer remarked that his tires seemed more worn than might be expected. Almost immediately came a shout from a spotter atop the Pagoda, "Car 59 is in trouble in the southeast turn . . . he has lost a wheel." With the loss of the wheel, the car rolled over and bounced along the wall, seriously injuring Granatelli and destroying the car.

RIGHT One of the strangest-appearing cars ever to show up at the Speedway arrived for the 1948 event . . . and it didn't do badly at all. It was called the Pat Clancy Special and was driven by Billy DeVore. The main idea of the six wheels was to give better traction and better handling. The four rear wheels were driven by two "midget type" rear axles, connected by a universal joint. The rest of the car was conventional, powered by a 270-cubic-inch Meyer-Drake engine. Although the car became the butt of many journalistic jokes, it qualified in the seventh row at a speed of 123.967 miles per hour, and it did appear to be rock-solid in the turns. Still running at the end, the car was flagged into 12th place, to become the first (and only) six-wheeled car ever to start and finish a 500-mile race.

BELOW This is a Mercedes-Benz racing car, a machine most mechanics claim is the worst in the world to try to maintain. Everything they must reach, they claim, is directly behind some other part which cannot be removed. The entire engine is a maze of wires and pipes and parts. Perhaps the Americans just hadn't learned the secret of the three-liter, 12-cylinder, S Mercedes, for again in 1948 (as in 1947) it did not do well. Chet Miller, who would eventually return to the Novi and lose his life, qualified this car in the seventh row of starters after Ralph Hepburn returned to his original Novi ride. But during the race, Chet suffered continual oil pressure problems (there are no fewer than **eight** oil pumps in the supercharged Mercedes S engine) and he was finally forced to drop out permanently on lap 108.

RIGHT Jimmy Jackson drove this Howard Keck Special in 1949 to a sixth-place finish in the 500-mile race. Jackson drove this Offenhauser-powered car the entire race without a pit stop, giving an indication of how tires had improved over the years of the "500." In fact, only nine tires were changed throughout the race, and only one of these (on Bill Holland's winning Blue Crown Spark Plug Special) was for other than mere precautionary reasons. Holland was showing some white ply when he came in for his change.

BELOW 1949 seemed to be the the "year" of the Novi. Twins were entered, one to be driven by hard-charging Rex Mays and this one to be driven by handsome Duke Nalon, who had previous experience in the Novi. The experience showed, for Nalon immediately captured the pole position for the race with a new record speed of 132.939 miles per hour. Mays followed up this performance by blasting his own Novi into the second-fast spot in the middle of the front row. Nalon jumped to an immediate lead and by the sixth lap he was passing the tail-enders. Rex Mays stayed right on his tail in the twin Novi, as the crowd cheered the two popular veterans on. But on lap 23, while leading going away, Nalon crashed violently and exploded in the northeast turn. He was able to crawl from the wrecked and burning Novi and walk to the ambulance. Soon after, on lap 48, Mays' engine quit, and both Novis were out for the year.

RIGHT Freddie Agabashian, a popular young driver, drove this Kurtis-Kraft, Inc. entry in the 1950 500-mile race. It was powered by a supercharged Offenhauser engine and appeared to be a contender in the race until it dropped out on lap 64 with a broken oil line.

BELOW Rookie Walt Faulkner, the "Little Dynamo," is shown here in the J. C. Agajanian-owned Grant Piston Ring Special. Faulkner passed his driver's test easily, then took the 270-cubic-inch Offenhauser-powered car and qualified at a new record speed of 134.343 miles per hour to take the pole position for the rain-shortened 1950 Indy race (won by Johnnie Parsons). The cam in this car was personally manufactured by Clay Smith, the chief mechanic, and is said to have accounted for the speed record, which included a new one-lap record speed of 136.013 miles per hour. In the race, which was called at 345 miles due to rain, Faulkner placed sixth to establish himself as a leading Indy contender in coming years. Nor would this be the last time the familiar "number 98" would dominate at Indy, for this Agajanian number would win twice in coming years.

RIGHT Italian champion Alberto Ascari took to the Indianapolis Motor Speedway reasonably well in this 12-cylinder Ferrari Special entered by Enzo Ferrari in 1952. Unfortunately the red and white car suffered a broken wire wheel in the northwest turn on lap 40, and spun into the infield out of the race. The car placed 31st in a field of 33 after starting in 19th position.

BELOW Lee Wallard, in a car which appeared to be little more than a stretched midget and with the smallest nonsupercharged engine in the 1951 "500," traded the lead with Jack McGrath during the first 50 miles of the race. But then Wallard began to build up a safe lead over the second-place car at the time, Mike Nazaruk, as more and more cars dropped out due to the very high temperature and the high speeds. Wallard's Offenhauser-powered Belanger Special (a Kurtis chassis) won the race with an average speed of 126.244 miles per hour.

RIGHT Still smarting from the 1952 "500," in which he hit the wall with only eight laps to go and while appearing a certain winner, Bill Vukovich, the "Mad Russian," hurtled his Fuel Injection Special to a new track record of 138.392 to take the pole position for the 1953 race. He did it in a driving rainstorm at that. Then, on race day, he sped his Offenhauser-powered roadster to a handy lead right from the start. Driving faster and faster on a terribly hot day while other drivers were spinning and crashing in an effort to keep up, Vukie led all but five laps of the race and was far, far ahead at the finish. It was one of the most convincing wins in the history of the "500"... and not the last one for the remarkable Vukovich.

BELOW The Cummins Diesel Company spent over one half million dollars on the design and development of this low-slung, six-cylinder oil burner, then assigned Freddie Agabashian to drive it in the 1952 "500." It lacked the "pick up" of the other cars in the race, but it really didn't need that during qualifications. Agabashian took the car out on the first day and set a new track record of 138.010 miles per hour to take the pole position for the start of the race. From that point on, however, things did not go so well for the sleek car. It dropped back at the start, and on lap 71 it suffered a clogged supercharger and dropped out of the race.

RIGHT Another streamlined entry in the 1955 race was this Jim Rathmann-driven Belond Special, constructed by Kurtis-Kraft after extensive wind tunnel tests of a model. The car was actually designed by well-known race car designer Quinn Epperly. It boasted a cutdown on wind drag of 50 per cent over the normal roadster. The main objective was to cut down air turbulence behind the wheels. Another unique feature on the car was its fully enclosed exhaust system, with the exhaust pipe running high along the inside of the body and out at the sharp tip of the streamliner's tail. Also tested on this car (but not used during the race) was a two-way radio in the headrest. The car finished in 14th place.

BELOW One of the most interesting cars in the 1955 race at Indianapolis was this super-streamlined Offenhauser-powered Sumar Special, driven by Jimmy Daywalt. It is shown here as it actually ran in the race, with the side body panels removed. The reason for the removal of the panels for the actual race was not so much for speed purposes, but because they hid the angle and the condition of the tires from driver Daywalt, and he felt less confident not being able to see these things. The side panels also contributed to a heating up of the disc brakes. Daywalt started in 17th position in the race, and finished in ninth place.

RIGHT Sam Hanks was a handsome veteran who had been trying to win the Indianapolis race since 1940, but it wasn't until 1957 that he teamed up with car builder George Salih. Salih's racer was a sleek Offenhauser-powered job with an Epperly chassis and a unique "lay down" engine design, where the engine was mounted on its side. The car was known as the Belond Exhaust Special, and looked fast just sitting on the grid. It was. Hanks won the 1957 race in the car with a new record speed of 135.601 miles per hour.

BELOW From first to last went Paul Russo and his Novi Vespa Special in the 1956 race at Indianapolis. Making still another bid for fame, the Novi Racing Corp., entered this supercharged eight-cylinder brute of a racing car and Russo qualified it in eighth position for the start. Almost immediately, to the great delight of the crowd, he thundered it into the lead and streaked away. But the happy spell was not to last for long, for on lap 22 Russo's car blew a tire and smashed into the wall in the southwest turn. The very first car out of the 1956 race, the Novi was placed 33rd at the finish.

RIGHT Another car to avoid the first-lap wreck in 1958 was the crowd-pleasing Novi, now known as the Novi Automobile Air Conditioner Special, but still driven by popular Paul Russo. However the car went out of the race on lap 122 with a leaking radiator and was placed in 18th position.

BELOW This bright yellow and red Offenhauser-powered roadster, entered as the Bob Estes Special and driven by Don Freeland, managed to avoid the first-lap carnage of the 1958 Indy race (in which 16 cars were involved and in which Pat O'Connor died). Starting in 13th position in the race, Freeland brought the Phillips-chassis racer home in seventh place.

◀ PREVIOUS PAGE After a three-year retirement from racing, driver Duane Carter returned to Indy in 1959. Things looked good for Carter, for he was assigned to drive this Smokey Yunick-built Offenhauser-powered racer (driven by Johnny Thomson in 1958), recently rebuilt with a brand new front end. Carter was the first man to qualify for the 1959 event after a perfect score in his familiarization tests (required due to his absence from racing). He drove a steady race and finished in seventh place to complete his comeback picture.

RIGHT The Demler Special was not new to the 500-mile race in 1960 having, in fact, an excellent previous record. It was driven by George Amick in 1958 after having been built that year by Quinn Epperly. Amick finished in second place. In 1959 it was driven by Paul Goldsmith and finished fifth. Here, in its 1960 configuration, the car is shown in the pits before the race. It is a laydown design (with the engine actually 18 degrees off true horizontal) with the engine on the left side of the car. The engine was a standard four-cylinder, 255-cubic-inch Offenhauser. In 1960 Goldsmith continued the fine record of the car by bringing it home in third place.

RIGHT. One of the most famous cars ever to run over the years at the Indianapolis Motor Speedway is this Watson-built, Offenhauser-powered roadster, #98, owned by J. C. Agajanian and driven by Parnelli Jones. The car was affectionately known as "Calhoun" and now rests in the Speedway Museum after a wonderful track career. The car is quite typical of the roadsters of the early sixties, for they all looked very much alike. Calhoun, however, under the guidance of Parnelli Jones, was different. Jones led the race in his very first "500" in 1961 in this car, eventually finishing in 12th place. In 1962, Jones broke the "150-mile-per-hour barrier" in Calhoun with a new record qualification speed of 150.370 mph. He was leading going away when brake line problems dropped him to a final finish of seventh. Jones and Calhoun won the 1963 500-mile race, and they were battling with eventual winner A. J. Foyt in 1964 when, during a pit stop, Calhoun caught fire and burned up. Experts restored the car for the museum, and Jones turned to the newer rear-engine models.

BELOW This car was the very beginning of a major revolution at Indy, though not many recognized it as such at the time. Jack Brabham, World Driving Champion in 1959 and 1960 and Australian-born, brought this small, lightweight Cooper Climax to Indy in 1961. The Climax engine was in the rear, but what was even worse to the American drivers, the car was painted a very "unlucky" green. The engine was by far the smallest in the field, a mere 168 cubic inches. The racer appeared almost to be a midget in a field of big cars. Its performance was not midget, however. Brabham drove a very steady, very consistent race and finished in ninth place . . . well ahead of many other standard American race cars.

RIGHT But the car that really finalized the revolution and steered everybody toward the rear engine style was this Lotus of Scotsman Jim Clark. Long, low, lean and cigar-shaped, this car was powered by a massive Ford V8 racing engine. Colin Chapman, the head of Lotus Cars, brought over an identical racer for Dan Gurney to drive, and the Americans watched the two cars carefully. They didn't have to look far to see this Lotus of Clark, for it dogged winner Parnelli Jones' heels, finally placing second by a scant margin. Gurney placed seventh, and the rear-engined cars were plainly here to stay. Frail-looking, they had proven themselves able to go the distance and remain competitive. They were smoother in the turns, and equal to the roadsters on the straightaways. The crowds liked them, no small consideration in American racing. The trend was obvious.

BELOW Mickey Thompson helped along the rear engine revolution at Indy by building and entering this stock block Buick-powered car in the 1962 event. International racing driver Dan Gurney qualified the car at 147.886 miles per hour for eighth starting position, and fans sat up and took notice. Many, many old faithful Offy roadsters did not do nearly this well. The eight-cylinder, rear-engined racer did well in the race until, on lap 92, a gear in the rear end snapped and the car dropped out. But the trend to rear engines had become more and more obvious.

RIGHT Returning in 1963 with a new car he had designed and built himself, and with Duane Carter as the driver, Mickey Thompson was confident. The car was the rear-engined Harvey Aluminum Special, powered by a stock block Chevrolet V8 engine. The car was a beautiful machine to look at, and it was fast as well. However, on lap 100 the engine threw a rod and the car was out of the race.

BELOW Painted rose, white and gold, and disguised as the Hotel Tropicana Special, the fabulous Novi reappeared in 1963. Eight cylinders of supercharged, whining, screaming power, and a bullet-shaped headrest, the car was entered by Novi, Inc., and driven by crowd-favorite Jim Hurtubise. The Novi luck hadn't changed much, though, for of the three Novis entered, not one finished. Bobby Unser's was the very first car out of the 1963 race when he spun his Novi on the second lap. Art Malone's Novi dropped out on lap 18 with clutch trouble, and Hurtubise finally dropped out on lap 102 with an oil leak.

Two brand new rear-engined racers for the 1964 500-mile race at Indy were the Eddie Sachs Red Ball Special, powered by Ford, and the Mickey Thompson-built Sears Allstate Special, powered by Ford and driven by Dave MacDonald. Sachs' car was more traditionally styled, while MacDonald's car was radically streamlined with wheel fairings and a flattened look. Both cars qualified easily, though not on the first day, so they were back in the field for the start. MacDonald was in the middle of the fifth row, and Sachs directly behind him in the middle of the sixth row. In the fourth turn on the second lap of the race MacDonald seemed to falter. He skidded sideways, bounced off the inside wall and shot to the center of the track with flames boiling from his car. Sachs, coming up from the rear at high speed and unable to stop, smashed directly into the MacDonald wreck and both cars exploded. Several other cars were wrecked in the flaming carnage, injuring their drivers. Sachs and MacDonald, both popular drivers, were killed. The rear-engine revolution had moved faster than safety precautions could follow, but immediately new restrictions followed this tragedy, including fuel and fuel cell regulations.

RIGHT In spite of the popularity of the rear-engined racers, A. J. Foyt chose to go one last time with his traditional "dying dinosaur" Watson-built, Offy roadster. He entered this car in the 1964 500-mile race, and he won.

BELOW Another brand new rear-engined racer built for the 1964 race was this Joe Huffaker-designed car with a rear-mounted Meyer-Drake engine. The car featured a liquid suspension system. It was qualified easily by Walt Hansgen, a rookie, at 152.581 miles per hour, and started in 10th position. By lap 50, Hansgen had moved the car into fourth place, but a long pit stop for new fuel injector jets dropped him out of contention. He finished in 13th place.

RIGHT By 1965, only six front-engined cars made the field for the 500-mile race. All the rest were rear-engined. One of the front-engined cars was the great Novi, now known as the STP Gasoline Treatment Special, sponsored by Andy Granatelli and driven by Bobby Unser. The car (shown here with a camera mounted over the cockpit for practice sessions) appeared big and bulky next to the small lightweights. This car, built on a Ferguson chassis, featured four-wheel-drive and the traditional eight-cylinder, supercharged Novi engine. Unser ran into oil line connector problems on lap 69, however, and dropped out of the race to finish in 19th position (after starting in eighth).

BELOW One of the most unusual appearing cars ever to show up at the Speedway was this Smokey Yunick designed and built "sidecar," shown here being tested by Duane Carter (who liked the car very much). Offenhauser powered, the Hurst Floor Shifter Special was built with a side compartment for the driver for better visibility, to improve weight distribution, and for better control. The car was wrecked by Bobby Johns during testing and it did not make the race.

RIGHT Built for the 1964 race by Rolla Vollstedt, this car had a Meyer-Drake (Offy) engine in the rear. The chassis was of space frame construction and offset to the left. Len Sutton drove the car in the 1964 "500," but a broken fuel pump casting put him out after 140 laps while he was running in fourth place. Shown here in the car is Billy Foster, a rookie, who started the 1965 race in the outside second row position. A broken water manifold put him out of the race after 85 laps and he officially finished in 17th place.

BELOW Another of the front-engined cars in the 1965 event was the Novi racer driven by Jim Hurtubise and known as the Tombstone Life Special. A Kurtis chassis, and standard two-wheel-drive, this car was also sponsored by STP and Andy Granatelli. The usual Novi luck held, and Hurtubise had barely completed one lap when he dropped out with transmission problems.

RIGHT Jackie Stewart, the fine Scottish driver, nearly won the 1966 Indianapolis 500-mile race in this Bowes Seal Fast Special, a Lola powered by Ford. Stewart was solidly in the lead with only 10 laps to go when an oil pressure problem forced him to drop out of the race. Graham Hill went on to win, becoming the first rookie in many years to win an Indy 500-mile race.

BELOW in 1965 Mickey Thompson once again reported in with a car entirely different in concept. Looking almost like a drag racer (a sport in which Thompson is famed), the metal-flake blue, metal-flake bronze and white racer was designed with its cockpit far to the rear and its engine up front, though the vast majority of the cars which made the field were of rear-engined design. Thompson powered his unique car with a modified Chevrolet V8 engine with the drive to the front wheels (the first front-drive at the Speedway in 10 years). Driver Bob Mathouser, shown here walking behind Thompson, encountered engine problems and the car failed to qualify for the race.

RIGHT Built on an Eisert chassis and powered by Ford was this Harrison Special driven by Ronnie Duman in the 1966 Indy "500." Chassis-builder Jerry Eisert also served as chief mechanic on the car. This beautiful gold, black and white car was another of those knocked out on the first lap of the 1966 "500."

BELOW Personally designed, built and driven by Dan Gurney was this 1966 Eagle powered by Ford. Gurney developed the Eagle at his All American Racers Inc., a race car development firm in Southern California. The car never had a chance to show what it could do in 1966, though, for it was involved in the fantastic 16-car smashup at the start, and never completed one lap.

RIGHT Coming back in 1967 with a new Eagle built by his own company, Dan Gurney qualified second fastest in the field for the middle front row position at the start. Powered by Ford and sponsored by Wagner Lockheed Brake Fluid, the car did very well until lap 160 when it dropped out with a burned piston.

BELOW One of the most unique cars to show up at Indy for the 1966 "500" was this twin-engined racer. It had a Porsche engine for the rear wheels, and another Porsche engine for the front wheels. Two engines can be used at Indy provided the total displacement of both does not exceed the displacement limit placed on all cars. To be driven by Bill Cheesbourg in the race, the car failed to qualify.

RIGHT A. J. Foyt had had a difficult time getting accustomed to the rear-engined cars, finally solving the last of his problems by designing and building his own racers. From his shop in Texas came this Ford-powered Coyote, custom made by Foyt for Foyt. And the gamble paid off, for in 1967 Foyt's strategy was to grab second place and then lie in wait for the failure of the Turbocar. As he had predicted, the turbine failed, and Foyt swept into the lead and under the checkered flag for his third win at Indianapolis.

BELOW Perhaps the most controversial racer ever to compete at Indy was this Andy Granatelli-owned STP Turbocar, driven by veteran Parnelli Jones. Powered by a turbine rather than a piston-type engine, the car skimmed silently around the track almost as though it were on rails. It qualified easily on the outside of the second row (as many accused Jones of "holding back") and at the start of the race promptly passed the five cars in front to glide to a handy lead. The four-wheel-drive of the car seemed to hold it solidly in the turns at any speed Jones chose to run, and the race appeared to be for second place. Rain fell early in the 1967 "500," postponing the race to the next day, but this didn't seem to make a bit of difference to the Jones Turbocar. It merely picked up where it left off the day before, increasing its lead easily as the others fought for second place far behind. The STP Oil Treatment Special appeared to be a certain winner when, with less than 10 miles of the original 500 to go, a small part failed in the gearbox and the car coasted into the pits and out of the race.

RIGHT This new V8-powered Brabham Repco racer, owned by Jack Brabham, qualified for the 1968 "500" with an average speed of 164.144 miles per hour with Vienna-born Jochen Rindt at the wheel. The car went out of the race, however, with a burned piston after only five laps of competition.

BELOW Based upon the success of the turbine in 1967, Andy Granatelli teamed with Colin Chapman to design and build a team of improved Turbocars for 1968. Long, low and wedge-shaped, the cars were just as controversial as the original Turbocar had been the year before. Some fans loved them, others hated them. Granatelli stayed with the proven four-wheel-drive technique, though he was forced to use a smaller turbine engine due to restrictions placed on this type of power by the staid United States Auto Club, sanctioning body at Indy. Chief driver of the STP team was Joe Leonard, shown here in the pole-winning car of 1968. Leonard seemed in complete command during the running of the race, though he did not lead many laps. He seemed to be content to run along in second or third place, directly behind the leaders, and most fans felt that this was his strategy. However, just as the year before, very near the end of the race, with Leonard finally solidly in the lead, a part failed in the fuel pump drive mechanism and Leonard coasted to a stop on the first turn safety apron. Bobby Unser, who had been Leonard's chief competition during the race, swept by the stalled Turbocar and under the checkered flag moments later.

RIGHT More turbines were being developed by other companies based upon the success of Parnelli Jones in 1967, even though Jones had not actually won the race. It was obvious that he had totally dominated it, however. One of the other companies was that of Carroll Shelby, who based his design on one very similar to the Jones turbine. The Shelby turbines were to be driven by Denis Hulme (shown here in the cockpit) and Bruce McLaren, but the cars were withdrawn for "safety" reasons before any qualification attempts, so the only turbines in the 1968 race were those of Granatelli/Chapman.

BELOW Dan Gurney's All American Racers built still another new Eagle for the 1968 500-mile race, as well as other Eagles for other drivers, for the design was becoming popular. Gurney chose to drive this stock block Ford V8, and qualified it at a speed of 166.512 miles per hour. Starting in 10th place, he finished second behind Bobby Unser, the only car on the same lap as the winner.

RIGHT Probably the real sentimental favorite of the fans was this front-engined roadster personally designed and built by its driver, Jim Hurtubise. The rear-engine revolution was complete, and the turbines seemed to be the new thing. Only Hurtubise, long a popular driver and a fan-favorite, had the nerve to enter a front-engined car. This car, called a Mallard, was specifically designed for Indianapolis, and Hurtubise felt it would restore the front-engine concept. It was powered by a turbocharged Offenhauser. The car was originally built for the 1967 race, but it was bumped from the lineup after Hurtubise qualified it. Qualified again in 1968, in 30th position at the start, the car went out after only nine laps with a burned piston.

BELOW Powered by a turbocharged Ford racing engine was this Lola car entered by Eric Broadley, and driven by the brother of the 1968 race winner, Al Unser. The car featured four-wheel-drive. Running with the leaders, Unser thundered into the first turn on the 41st lap and halfway through he lost a wheel. Instantly the car smashed into the outside wall and skidded along it for many yards. Although Al was not injured, the car was almost totally demolished.

◀ **PREVIOUS PAGE** This Jack Adams Airplane Special was one of the new wedge-shaped, piston-powered cars designed especially for the 1969 race at Indianapolis, and patterned after the successful shape of the 1968 Turbocars. It was powered by a turbocharged Offenhauser engine, and driven by veteran Jim McElreath. The car qualified seventh fastest in the field for the inside of the third row at the start. Early in the race, though, the car caught fire as it screamed down the long straightaway. Instantly aware of the heat boiling up from behind him, McElreath coolly steered the car down the straightaway and up out of the groove in the first turn, out of the way of the other racers. There, finally, he unbuckled his seat belts and jumped clear as firemen rushed up to put out the by-then fierce fire. The car was badly burned and out of the race.

RIGHT The single turbine-powered car in the 1969 field of entries was this Jack Adams Special. It conformed, so it was thought, to the newest restrictions of USAC with regard to this type of power. It was entered and listed as having an annulus inlet area of 12.5 square inches. Veteran Al Miller barely qualified the car in the starting field, only to have it bumped by a faster car on the final day of qualifications. Finally, to once and for all stop any further invasion of turbines, USAC measured the engine of this car and promptly banned it from the track as not meeting the annulus inlet specifications. Not that it really mattered, anyhow, except to kill the controversial turbines once and for all.

RIGHT One of the few owner-drivers in the 1969 race was Californian George Follmer, shown here standing in his Retzloff Chemical Special turbocharged Ford racer. Follmer qualified the car at a speed of 164.286 miles per hour to start in the outside, ninth row position. The car dropped out of the race on the 26th lap with mechanical difficulties.

BELOW This Brabham Repco shown here with developer and driver Jack Brabham, was entered in the 1969 "500" at Indianapolis. It was powered by an eight-cylinder unblown (non-supercharged) 254.3-cubic-inch Repco Brabham engine. The car started the race in the middle of the 10th row, but dropped out on lap 58 with mechanical problems.

RIGHT Art Pollard, a veteran, drove this Andy Granatelli-owned STP Oil Treatment Special in the 1969 race at Indianapolis. A four-wheel-drive car, it was powered by a turbocharged Offenhauser engine. Pollard qualified the car on the outside of the fourth row with a speed of 167.123 miles per hour, but the car only lasted seven laps before it dropped out of the race.

BELOW Another wedge-shaped car designed for the 1969 race was this Arnie Knepper-driven M.V.S. Special. The car was powered by a turbocharged Ford racing engine and qualified on the outside of the seventh row. Knepper was doing well in the race until he brushed the wall along the main straightaway on lap 83, lost a wheel and came to rest directly in the middle of the track with oncoming racers hurtling toward him at high speed. Knepper stood up in his car and waved the others around one side or the other through the dust of the crash rather than running for the safety of the wall.

RIGHT The "Rookie of the Year" for 1969 was Mark Donohue. He drove this Sunoco Special, a four-wheel-drive turbocharged Offenhauser, finishing in seventh place in the race. Donohue had qualified fourth fastest in the field with a speed of 168.903 mph.

BELOW An extreme wedge shape marked this Thermo-King Special driven by Gary Bettenhausen, son of the great Tony Bettenhausen, in the 1969 Indy race. One of the fastest cars in the field, it started from the outside of row three, but lasted only 35 laps before it dropped from the race with mechanical problems.

RIGHT The hero of the 1969 race was Mario Andretti. He had available to him a four-wheel-drive racer which was brand-new and especially built for the 1969 race, but he smashed it against the fourth turn wall during practice destroying the car completely and injuring himself with facial burns. With no other choice, he turned to this year-old Brawner Hawk STP Oil Treatment Special powered by a turbocharged Ford engine. It was a car he had raced along the Championship Trail, but one not expected to have a chance at the "500." Mario qualified the car second fastest in the field for the middle of the front row of starters, and from there he dominated the race. Putting down challenges by A. J. Foyt and others, Mario drove a perfectly consistent race to win by almost three laps to the great delight of fans around the world . . . and to the even greater delight of car owner Andy Granatelli, who had been trying for 23 years, as a driver, mechanic and owner, to win the Indianapolis Speedway Race. Mario's victory was one of the most popular in the history of the great classic, and one of the most well-deserved. For his victory, Mario won a new record prize of $206,727.06 total.

BELOW Returning with still another newly designed Eagle built by All American Racers, Dan Gurney qualified this Olsonite Eagle into the fourth row of starters with a speed of 167.341 miles per hour. For power, Gurney chose his own Gurney Eagle stock block Ford engine, unblown. The car did extremely well in the race, battling for the lead all the way. It finally finished in second place to firmly establish the Eagle as a competitive racing car (especially since Bobby Unser had won in an Eagle the year before).

Index
cars and drivers

Abels Auto Ford Special, 72
Agabashian, Freddie, 101, 104
Alley, Tom, 41
Andretti, Mario, 155
Anel, 26
Apperson, 14
Arbuthnot, R. M. W., 87
Ascari, Alberto, 103
Bailey, George, 79
Bandini, Robert, 39
Barringer, George, 86
Belanger Special, 102
Belond Special, 107, 109
Bender, 41
Bergere, Cliff, 66, 91
Bettenhausen, Gary, 152
Blue Crown Spark Plug Special, 88, 92, 93
Bob Estes Special, 110
Boillot, Andre, 44
Bowes Seal Fast Special, 67, 83, 85
Boyle Special, 80-81
Brabham, Jack, 116, 148
Brabham Repco, 139, 148
Brawner Hawk STP Oil Treatment Special, 155
Bugatti, 47
Burd Piston Ring Special, 76
Burman, Bob, 29
"Calhoun," 117
Camco Special, 90
Carter, Duane, 112-113, 121, 126
Case, 16-17, 21
Chandler, 37
Cheesbourg, Bill, 134
Chevrolet, Gaston, 43
Chiron, Louis, 61
Chitwood, Joie, 95

Christiaen, Josef, 38
Chromolite Special, 59
Clark, Jim, 119
Cooper Climax, 116
Cooper, Earl, 36, 51, 54
Corum, Lora L., 56
Coyote, 137
Crawford, 37
Cummins, 64, 69, 104
Daywalt, Jimmy, 106
DeCystria, Prince, 47
Delage, 34
Delage Special, 61
Demler Special, 115
DePalma, Ralph, 24, 35, 53
DeVore, Billy, 97
DeVore, Earl, 59
Disbrow, Louis, 21
Donohue, Mark, 153
Duesenberg, 13, 46, 53
Duesenberg Straight-8, 45
Duman, Ronnie, 133
Durant, Cliff, 55
Duray, Leon, 60
Eagle, 132, 135, 140, 154
Eldridge Special, 57
Endicott, Bill, 23
Endicott, Harry, 25
Evans, Dave, 64, 69
Fageol Twin Coach Special, 84
Faulkner, Walt, 100
Ferrari Special, 103
Firestone-Columbus, 22
Follmer, George, 149
Foster, Billy, 129
Foyt, A. J., 125, 137
Frayer, Lee, 22
Freeland, Don, 110

Fuel Injection Special, 105
Gilmore Special, 68, 70
Goldsmith, Paul, 115
Granatelli, Andy, 94
Grant Piston Ring Special, 100
Gulotta, Tony, 76
Gurney, Dan, 118, 132, 135, 140, 154
Guyot, Albert, 30, 34
Hanks, Sam, 109
Hansgen, Walt, 124
Harrison Special, 133
Harroun, Ray, 18
Hartz, Harry, 58
Harvey Aluminum Special, 121
Hattel, Karl, 72
Haupt, Willie, 28
Hawkes, W. D., 57
Hepburn, Ralph, 83, 89
Holland, Bill, 92
Horn, Ted, 71
Householder, Ronney, 78
Howard Keck Special, 99
Hudson, 40
Hughes, Hughie, 15
Hulme, Denis, 141
Hurst Floor Shifter Special, 126
Hurtubise, Jim, 120, 128, 143
Jack Adams Airplane Special, 144-145
Jack Adams Special, 147
Jackson, Jimmy, 99
Jones, Parnelli, 117, 136
Junior 8, 52
Keeton, 29
Knepper, Arnie, 150
Knox, 20
Kurtis-Kraft, Inc. 101
Lagonda, 87
LeCocq, Louis, 39
Leonard, Joe, 138
Lewis, Dave, 52

Liesaw, R. C., 26
Locomobile Special, 55
Lola, 131, 142
Lotus, 119
Lytle, Herbert, 14
McDonald, J. C., 62
McElreath, Jim, 144-145
McGurk, Frank, 72
McQuinn, Harry, 77
M.V.S. Special, 150
MacDonald, Dave, 122
Mallard, 143
Marchese Special, 77
Marmon, 19, 73
Maserati, 74, 80-81
Mason, 28
Mathouser, Bob, 130
Mays, Rex, 85
Mercedes, 24, 35, 48-49
Mercedes-Benz, 96
Mercedes-Knight, 29
Mercer, 15, 31
Meyer, Lou, 63
Miller, 54, 71, 79
Miller, Al, 147
Miller, Chet, 96
Miller, Eddie, 45
Miller, Erskine, 58
Miller Special #4, 60
Monroe, 43
Mulford, Ralph, 20
Murphy, Jimmy, 45
Nalon, Duke, 98
Novi, 83, 89, 91, 98, 108, 111, 120, 127, 128
Nyborg, 25
Nyquist Special, 95
Oldfield, Barney, 32
Oldfield, Lee, 73
Pat Clancy Special, 97
Pawl, John, 76

Petillo, Kelly, 70
Peugeot, 42
Pillete, Theodore, 29
Pollard, Art, 151
Rathmann, Jim, 107
Red Ball Special, 122
Reo Royale, 66
Retzloff Chemical Special, 149
Rickenbacker, Eddie, 33
Rindt, Jochen, 139
Roamer, 39
Romcevich, Pete, 90
"Romthe" Special, 62
Rose, Mauri, 88
Russo, Paul, 84, 108, 111
STP Oil Treatment Special, 151
STP Turbocar, 136, 138
Sachs, Eddie, 122
Sailer, Karl, 48-49
Sampson, Alden II, 63
Schacht, 23
Schmidt, Special, 56
Schneider, Louie, 67
Sears Allstate Special, 122

Shafer, Red, 65
Shaw, Wilbur, 75, 80-81
Shelby Turbine, 141
Sparks-Thorne Special, 78
Stapp, Babe, 74
Stewart, Jackie, 131
Strang, Lewis, 16-17
Stubblefield, Stubby, 68
Studebaker Special, 51
Stutz, 32, 36
Summer Special, 106
Sunbeam, 30, 38, 44
Sunoco Special, 153
Talbot-Darracq, 44
Thermo-King Special, 152
Tucker Torpedo Special, 86
Unser, Al, 142
Unser, Bobby, 127
Vail, Ira, 40
Vukovich, Bill, 105
Wallard, Lee, 102
Whalen, Neil, 21
Wilcox, Howard "Howdy," 42
Wishart, Spencer, 31